MATTHEW FRA...

Dragons

ff

faber and faber

First published in 2001
by Faber and Faber Limited
3 Queen Square London WC1N 3AU
Published in the United States by Faber and Faber, Inc.,
an affiliate of Farrar, Straus and Giroux, New York

Typeset by Faber and Faber Ltd
Printed in England by MPG Books Limited,
Victoria Square, Bodmin, Cornwall

A CIP record for this book
is available from the British Library

ISBN 0–571–20666–2

10 9 8 7 6 5 4 3 2 1

Contents

Acknowledgements

Acknowledgement is due to the following publications in which some of these poems first appeared: *City Writings*, *Gathering Swallows*, *PN Review*, *Poetry London*, *Poetry Review*, *Stand*, *The Rialto*, *The Times Literary Supplement*, *Venta*, *The Waterlog*.

'Ocean' was commissioned by the Poetry Society for its Website (*http://www.poetrysoc.com*) as part of the Poetry Places Scheme. It was written during an enjoyable and productive stay at Hawthornden Castle, Scotland. Most of the factual content, as well as the narrative structure and one or two evocative phrases, are drawn from the essay 'A Walk on the Deep Side: Animals in the Deep Sea' by P. A. Tyler, A. L. Rice, C. M. Young and A. Gebruk in *Oceanography: An Illustrated Guide*, edited by C. P. Summerhayes and S. A. Thorpe (Manson Publishing, 1996), and other details come from essays in the same book.

'The Ornamental Hermit' won the TLS/Blackwell's Prize, 2000.

'City Autumn' won the Gathering Swallows Prize for the best poem by a published poet in response to Keats's 'To Autumn'.

The eight Winchester poems were commissioned by Winchester City Council for a walking tour of the city as part of its Celebration of Literature, 1999.

The four forest poems were written during a residency in the New Forest arranged by the New Forest Poetry Society under the auspices of the Poetry Society's Poetry Places Scheme.

Thanks to Christina Patterson and the Poetry Society; the Director, Administrator and Trustees of the Hawthornden Foundation; Paul Tyler and staff of Southampton Oceanography Centre; Keiren Phelan and Southern Arts; Sally Edwards and Winchester City Council; Keith and Pam Bennett, Moira Clark and the New Forest Poetry Society; the many friends and colleagues who have given me support and feedback; and, as always, to Creina.

Dragons

Dragons

It was not the ideal day to go looking for dragons –
drizzly. You want it crisp, what you call dragons'
weather. They stay inside when it's wet. Dragons
are great ones for forty winks. There must be dragons
snoring underneath us this minute in the old dragons'
tunnels. All right, Craig, let's go. We got in the Dragons
Unlimited Land Cruiser and set off into the Dragons
Range foothills, just four of us, shivering, and the two Dragons
Agency registered guides Craig and Dylan, who said he saw dragons'
spoors in the mud and knelt down muttering, dragons
were here all right, two females and some halfgrown dragons.
See, the bracken's charred where the yearling dragons
were playburning. You don't get that with the bull dragons –
when they flame they mean it. I've seen dragons –
Dylan, it's gone ten and these people are after dragons.
Those cinder droppings are stone cold. The dragons
will be miles away by now. We looked at each other. Dragons
seemed unlikely in the grey drip but Dylan smelled dragons
so we slithered up the road and found a field where dragons
had rutted. It looked like scramblers but Dylan said dragons.
In any case the ruts were still there but not the dragons
so we ate our sandwiches while the guides talked dragons
and sheep burnings and farmsteads torched by dragons
and places you couldn't grow dahlias for the dragons –
the colours seem to enrage them – and how male dragons

display at night on the summits. I've been here when dragons
lit up the sky for miles – it was just like the dragons
talking to each other in firework morse, dash dot dash. Dragons
don't burn so hot as they used to and some dragons
have gone out completely, from the conditions. Imagine, dragons
extinct. It was all too easy. The afternoon was white now, dragons
out of the question, so we climbed back into Dragons
Unlimited and Craig drove us back down saying, I saw dragons
only last week, a small one anyway. As for us we saw dragons
all the way, a nostril sculpted in shiny rock, a twist of dragon's
breath in the fog, the stunted vestigial dragons'
wings in a crest of dry-stone wall. Dylan said dragons
are like that. Sometimes you see them everywhere, dragons.

Ocean

Margin

You're nearly there at last. The ocean is in the air,
although you can't see it yet. The sheep-grazed contours
now have an edge to them, as if the next field
might drop away into nothing. You've stared

at the distance so long it dissolves
into the swimming of your eyes,
a blue tremble. Is it you

or is that a fault-line
on the horizon,

a second sky?

∙๑

People who live close to the sea get shrivelled by it.
They cultivate nets, parched ropes and grey splintered wood,
essences of tar, seaweed and bird-droppings,
orange plastic and blistering front doors.

This is the dry land the tide guzzles
that even the shivery rain
can never reconstitute.

Gulls like detached waves are
its emblem, doodled

in the margin.

5

They woke you this morning regurgitating their cries
and you went for a walk unravelling yourself
till you finally arrived at a loose end.
Only the sea knew where it was going.

This evening the girls are all dressed up,
glitter on the cobbles, the dark
slipping from their bare shoulders.

Prom night. They huddle near
its unseen body

breathing away.

⋙

So you got here, then. You're staying in a B and B
with sea view. You've eaten fish and chips on the beach
and had your fortune told: she saw a journey –
and you'd thought this was the end of the road.

A long way. Not in a boat. Not France,
much deeper. Are you getting warm?
You'll be colder soon. And dark.

Not death. More like going
back where you came from

and don't belong.

Shallows

First on the beach. Not even a jogger about yet.
The sand is touched with red light and chills your ankles
as you stagger from leg to leg undressing.
You leave your clothes for it to settle in,

and cross the strand with its lugworm casts
and plazas of sculpted ripples
to a sea turning over

in its sleep. Last night's blue
is still here, waiting,

reaching for you.

❧

At first it's all fizz and you have to step in it twice
because it keeps going back on you: touch and go,
but then it makes friends. You could get used to this –
or rather the shallows have warmed to you.

The test is when it reaches your leg
or, worse, your groin. Or when it burns
a purple line round your waist.

When it grabs your shoulders.
When you duck under

and your heart stops.

❧

It's blue and it's up and it's salty and it's down and
it's green and it's in your mouth and it's up and it's
blue and it's in your eyes and you can't see and
it's up your nostrils and you can't breathe and

it's an atmosphere you're standing on
and a solid you're seeing through
and a colour you're breathing.

You stand on the bottom.
You see blue and green.

You breathe water.

It isn't enough to have your sea-legs. You will need
sea-eyes to open the dark, sea-lungs to sponge up
oxygen, and a sea-skin to protect you
in the cold crushing place you're heading for.

Set out for the deep, past the headland
where the rocks grip leather ribbons
of kelp. Just above your head

the air is gatecrashing.
The tide's coming in

as you go out.

Shelf

You may be out of your depth, but not out of the world.
This is where most of it is. In the blue sunshine,
in the green fogs of plant bits, the water winds
that ripple the sand here too, you're walking

still close to home. It's like the rockpool
of your dreams, where anemones
don't turn out to be weeds, crabs

can still move, and there are
fumbling galaxies

of five-armed stars.

જ

So many animals leave themselves lying around.
A doormat-sized plaice covered in mud, its features
laid out on top, nearly trips you. A scallop
squirts away like a startled paperweight.

There's no waymarking. You move your feet
at your own risk. The sea urchins
and whelks were before you, slow

knobbly crawlers. You walk
on their sluggish land

with fish for birds.

જ

If you could you'd be a herring, one among many,
making your home in movement, squeezed by everyone
you'd ever known, letting the world slip away
over your flanks, holding yourself in tight

to fire like a bullet through your life,
eating and breathing where you went,
knowing only silver and

not-silver, a terror
of dolphins, a wrenched

halt in the net.

You had got used to the unlikely swimming-pool blue
downwelling from the surface, how it made the fish
into shimmers of water, twisting away
and vanishing as you reached out your hand.

Now you've arrived in evening, where each
step takes you further from the light.
You have to look for it first

before you see with it.
You will reach night soon.

Blue stars drift past.

Slope

This is the road from the shelf to the abyssal plain.
Its name is mud. So let's see how low we can get,
exploring the local night-life. This red crab
rearing up at you with his pincers splayed

thinks you're invading his territory,
the city of mounds and burrows
where crabs hang out, on the edge.

Don't stir up sediment.
Just sidle past him

down the soft slope.

&

You cross a knee-high forest of feathers, the sea-pens
filtering granules of food from the slow currents
that push through the dark. They finger you as if
regretting you're too big for them to eat.

You pass the sponge-fields where hairy pots
the size of grapefruit are half-sunk
in the mud, breathing through holes

in their tops, a trove no
archaeologist

will excavate.

&

Where you come from a cucumber is a vegetable
that tastes of green pondwater. But the ones here have
a will of their own. This one's a spiky tube
flexing itself on its nipples of legs;

another's its own magic carpet,
a living shoe-sole that billows
over the sea-floor, lightly

as if its tons of sky
were not pressing it,

grazing the ooze.

How long has it been snowing? You've only just noticed
the scatter of flakes falling round you, but you know
that's it's gone on and will go on forever
and that it always settles. You catch one.

It isn't any colder than you
in your miles-deep chill. It won't melt
after its fall through the wet.

It's a piece of something
that was once alive,

a being flake.

Abyss

Now at last you've reached the flat lands, the abyssal plain
where sea cucumbers have scrawled their tracks on the floor
for you to read. No current wipes them away.
Whatever lives here has the steadiness

of lowlanders; they scrape out burrows,
live on the leavings of above,
make their own entertainment.

As you pass through their fields,
they chat about you

in blue morse code.

        ❧

News from the surface. It has been spring there recently
and the plankton has flowered, a drifting forest.
Specks of animals sheltered and browsed in it,
left their droppings, and died when the plants died,

and the whole tangle of tissue sank.
Now the lowlanders have their turn,
a hand-me-down flowering

that fills the hollows with
edible, green-brown,

flocculent gunge.

        ❧

This was a sperm whale that swam with outriding dolphins,
that hung from the swell to sleep, disturbed the ocean
as it plunged into the darkness to hunt squid.
It is deeper than ever now, opened

and stinking, the squid's parroty beaks
spilled out on the floor. The red shrimp
and rat-tail fish tear the white

from its last rags of blue.
It will be gone soon,

a weight lifted.

જ

Just when you thought you had no enemies here, something
stabs your foot. You think of seasnakes and weever fish –
what venoms have been waiting under the sludge
to kill their first ever human? You stoop

and pull out a tapered length of rust.
The tab on the end shows a ship.
It reads: SS *Madeira*.

Once on the sun-deck this
held the cherry in

a manhattan.

Ridge

These mountains have no echoing views, no vertigo.
You climb them intimately, gripping the rockface
in a tight-fitting and protective blackness.
It's hard to remember how far you've come –

thinking only in fingers and toes
you seem to be climbing yourself
from the inside. But you're not.

This is the ridge that runs
through all the oceans,

the world's Great Wall.

ఌ

Having crossed the mountains where no anemone grows
you reach the median valley. From the last slope
you sense some hidden activity, and smell
burning as if someone had lit a fire

to welcome you at your journey's end.
The rock chimneys are abandoned,
streaky with rust and blue paint

but work is going on
where the shrimp cluster

like bees swarming.

ఌ

This black smoker might be one of the chimneys of hell,
blurring the darkness with gushing sulphur, scalding
the cold water that's too heavy to boil off.
These shrimp are like complicated pink souls,

jostling in the tormented water,
driven mad by their own numbers,
goaded by the claws of crabs.

And is this what souls eat,
this white matted stuff,

manna from hell?

        ❧

Listen. The ocean is draining into the fissures
and simmering in the hot earth, all the ocean,
a kettleful at a time. It makes black smoke
that feeds the white bacteria. You watch

the earth and ocean becoming life,
the matted stuff shrimp are made of –
and crabs and sea cucumbers,

starfish, anemones,
whales, the whole rockpool,

including you.

Surface

Where you came from is one thing, but where are you going?
You can't stay here by the chimney. It's time to leave.
Float up with the smoke through the water column.
Perhaps there are larvae floating with you,

glass slivers primed to look for the heat
of the next vent so that the shrimp
don't die out when their fire does.

They'll only come so far.
You seek your own fire,

the yellow one.

๑

You go from down to up, decompressing all the time
with a splutter as your sea-breath goes out of you,
startling an oarfish, a red-maned sea-serpent
that loops round opening its toothless mouth.

The sea's still too dark, indigo with
the wrong gleam in its many eyes.
Plankton are upwelling too,

a snowfall in reverse
towards the snowlight

of the surface.

๑

You come up in the magnesium of a full moon,
getting your sunlight secondhand for the moment.
You must have been walking all day in the dark.
Now that your head is out of the water

you realize how far from home you are –
the moon could be the nearest land.
Where wind and sea meet, you feel

cold in two ways at once.
But keep on treading.

The boat will come.

     ✿

The surface of the ocean. It's too deep here for waves.
There is only the slight swell that turns into them
thousands of miles away. A bubble rises,
which you'd never notice, except this time

you're closer to it than you might be
and have been to where it came from.
Now it's dispersed in the air –

another ocean, or
part of the same one,

the deep blue world.

City Autumn

Offices have no seasons. This morning,
as every Thursday, two maintenance women
sprayed the unchanging leaves of our atrium rainforest.
We had another rainforest, wet coats by the door.

But sometimes I almost think a leaf-toast smell
winds itself into the air-conditioning.
The day closes early. I stand at the window
watching the lava of rear lights ooze its way home.

Autumn: a place between stations. In the subways
young men sit stiff-legged as guys, asking for pennies.
And once I came out of the tube to find the sky
a whirl of commuter black, the swallows passing through.

Autumn Noir

The kid slipped into a bar. I looked through the window.
It was all potted palms, baby flesh and cigarette smoke
like a rainforest kindergarten for infants with bad habits.
I would be about as inconspicuous there as a fishfinger in a plate of
    bouillabaisse.

The kid sucked his girl's neck under a yucca
between drinks. Last year's fashion was limes.
I was wishing I'd worn my coat. I could smell
onions somewhere and something beyond onions

like leaves burning far away as if there was a kind of smoke
that belonged in the air, that the world made on its own.
Maybe that's what I was following all along, the scent of autumn.
Meanwhile the kid had vanished. His girl sipped at a drink the
    colour of stop lights on a wet road. She didn't seem to like it.

Postmodern Autumn

Were it indeed possible to think a season externally to the panoply
    of mists and apples, of fructuality,
such a depanoplized season would instantly re-extend to us in a
    graceful gesture
its refructified self as shell and kernel at the same time, a nut as
    both case and history.
We have always probably not exactly cracked it.

This is our reappropriation of the granary
from the ejaculatory oozings of men's quills,
our investment in harvest, our gleaning of difference, our
    unwinnowed hair, our
carelessness, frankly. It's about bodies.

The pleasure of the sign, of the seen, of the sin,
of the son/sun, of the spring, of the unstrung,
of the thing that, of the think not, of the thin gnat,
of the singifier and the singified, of the sing. Questions? Drinks?

Leafstory

The park is not green but
yellow today, buried
underneath fidgety
leaves I trash with my feet –

more of them than the trees'
scrawny posing suggests.
Exhaling earthiness,
as if from down not up,

they might be the whole world's
soggy party nibbles,
surprising evidence
that we still live where all

the books are set, that years
decay, weather affects
everything, entities
that eat sun still shit gold.

Frog Chronicle

1

These two round objects which are known as *tomes*
produce the *gollum*, which is passed through here
along the *inkling*, which as of course you know
is the same conduit used for passing water.

Before this happens the inkling must be aroused.
It extends to at least two and a half times its normal length,
which is called an *allusion* as I expect you knew.
He was bald and sweating with embarrassment.

And so we saw ourselves as doctors see us,
a pant-shaped diagram of butchery red
and the sawdust-yellow walls of organs. Yes,
we'd had an inkling. Tomorrow we'd do women.

2

Arousal must take place in both parties
before the *frogging*, which is the pushing of
the alluded inkling into the *bermuda*,
culminating in the eventual *binge*.

The bermuda was an estuary of red
in a map whose outlines recalled our own.
The *fritillary* was labelled like a city,
almost invisible among the marshes.

Arousal would take place there in one party.
I tried to picture the map becoming human,
the fritillary nestling among its folds
ready to startle. Would something in me know how?

3

The lessons had left something to be desired.
I saw women now as if for the first time,
the slight weight of a *partridge* against a blouse,
the profile of a *nephew* seen through cloth,

Surrogate Wife read in a darkened classroom.
That son of a bitch never tickled his wife's fritillary.
The poor cow didn't know what she was missing.
Gently like this. Yes yes etc.

My list of things deferred grew a few inches.
I put the book on the shelf just after marriage
but before death. They were still too tall to kiss
but one day we would turn into a frog.

4

Night was full of the flapping of partridges.
My bed was Plato's cave. I could see in the dark
and my hands felt for the plump, the delicate.
I travelled to an imaginary bermuda

in the scent of Mycil ointment, then of gollum.
I thought for years that I'd invented it.

The teacher had said playing. This was serious.
At school I was too respectable to be told.

I found it one day in the dictionary.
Kindle. To produce a binge in self or another
by manual excitation of the *registers.*
They were laughing in the cave. It was open house.

5

I realized I was already behindhand.
It wasn't frogging I pined for so much
as what was supposed to come before it, kissing,
an arm round her in the pictures. It was normal,

and normal was looking increasingly unlikely.
The despair of the mirror, a sag of a face
and a body like a prawn. Nights in the cave,
the sheen of gollum on the morning sheets,

as one by one they leave their desks and go
to the places after school where the world waits
smiling, holding a girlfriend by the hand.
There are worse griefs but none so embarrassing.

6

Call her Amanda. I met her at a party
and shortly before morning I was too tired
to care if she rejected me. My arm
cradled her shoulders and we both forgot it.

Saturdays on the couch. I unpeeled her dress
and slipped a gentle partridge out of its cup.
Her nephew was a baby, pink and shy.
She whispered put it back and made me want to.

A nice girl didn't frog nice boys like me.
I became expert at putting the partridge back,
a sort of unpetting. Nice was no good.
At least one of us had to be nasty.

7

Amanda fizzled out. I was still a *cherub*,
a word I always hated for its soft
scriptural overtones, a word for girls.
For me cherubhood was an albatross.

They can smell a cherub coming. They know
by the way my voice goes up at the end of a sentence?
I'll never live it down. A cherub's walk,
a cherub's way of drinking beer and not

enough of it. The girls I knew by now
treated me as a pet. I flopped on their floors
pretending to be drunk. They shooed me out
when their lovers came, the tall uncherubim.

8

Call her Michelle but only in the week.
Weekends she spent with a businessman in Chingford

who was married Monday to Friday. You have to know
that I'm really a very emotional person.

I only frog a man I really love.
I would never give it away. I won't be used.
We kissed on the carpet. The partridges,
which were large and docile, stayed in their cage.

The great thing about love, it makes you intimate
with those you haven't met. I wanted to kill him
or at least bite her neck one Friday for him
but typically I never had the tomes.

9

I know the secret of the cherubim.
There isn't one. The worst part of it is
that there is no one you can tell it to.
I wished that I was less of a man or more

instead of more or less. It's easy to speak
of something that's a kind of speech itself.
You never tell the things you never do.
There were no maps to show how I remained

in the same place I'd started, ordinary
without a hope of striking out for normal,
a state I hardly imagined any more.
You've been a cherub. You know how it is.

And call her Beth and call this somewhere else.
Talking of T. S. Eliot in a bar
with dogwoods outside the window, a southern spring.
I think it's time I ventured an allusion.

I call this somewhere else. Two margaritas
and it's still daylight. This is the happy hour.
I lick the salt from my lips and gaze into
my jamjar glass full of a cloudy liquid.

It tastes like nothing on earth. It's not surprising
as this is the happy hour and somewhere else.
I catch myself being obscenely charming.
They speak a different body language here.

Like getting on a train to nakedness.
One minute we were there and the next in
an X-rated movie of our own devising.
After waiting all those years it was too sudden

and her nephews' presence was embarrassing.
I found my first bermuda in the flesh,
exactly like a diagram of itself.
The maps I saw must have been made by women.

I had no trouble getting an allusion
but a binge was beyond me. It didn't matter.
I had the freedom of the species now.
The words flew to their meanings: woman, frog.

Tomes. The great authors ponderously bound.
Gollum. A creature of slime or slime of creatures.
Inkling. The part of a man that gets allusions.
Allusion. That which points beyond oneself.

Fritillary. The fluttering part of a woman.
Bermuda. Where a cherub goes to die.
Partridge. Extremely sought-after kind of game.
Nephew. A small intruder (masculine: *niece*).

Kindle. To rub an inkling till it whooshes.
Binge. A whole hoard of feelings splurged at once.
Registers. How we know who we are thinking.
Cherub. An unfallen angel in the void.

Frog. Low-level bouncer, leggy and primeval.
Frog Chronicle. A place where frogs are told.

What the Cuttlefish Do

Who's the girl you saw on the beach?
Is she the girl for you?
The backs of her knees are marked with an H,
her breasts are a W.

You've taken her to a hot, bright dance,
to the cold cliffs in the rain.
You've laid your arm on her shoulders
and taken it off again.

You talked over coffee and biscuits,
you talked over cakes and tea,
and both of you knew you were going to do
what the cuttlefish do in the sea.

They have a faceful of feelers,
which gives them a worried air,
and their bodies are bags of ocean,
with a skirt all round to steer.

They know how to change colour
and they know how to make love.
The female trembles underneath,
the male trembles above.

He's passed her a gobbet of pearl drops.
She's glued her eggs to a weed.
They swam off side by side and quietly died,
having planted the cuttlefish seed.

And you know that if you have to
there's a quiet hotel you can go
where you can tremble on top of her
and she can tremble below.

She has a W and an H
and a Y between her legs.
When you've read it all night you may answer it right –
you do it because of the eggs.

If you really really had to,
you would do it till you were both dead –
leave the embryo, like the cuttlefish do,
glued to the foot of the bed.

Bath

A china canyon, miles of gleam. You slip
on curving cliffs that sweat a liquid light,
and all the legs you have can't get a grip.

Too dizzy now, you cannot find the lip
of the dark hole that opened into white,
a china canyon, miles of gleam. You slip,

and somewhere at your back you hear the drip
of detonating water. All your might
and all the legs you have can't get a grip.

You ford the estuary, a rougher strip
pocked by fierce cleansers. The horizon's bright,
a china canyon, miles of gleam. You slip

on the far side. A crash. You almost flip.
A glacier jamjar trawls for you. Hold tight!
But all the legs you have can't get a grip.

Coaxed by a thunderbolt of fingertip,
you face the hard clear void. To left and right,
a china canyon, miles of gleam. You slip
and all the legs you have can't get a grip.

Late June

As soon as the heat starts,
neighbour murmurs, sprinklers,
barbecue aromas,
permeability.

And the deaf man leaves his
window open, TV
rebounding everywhere –
Wimbledonmania.

Nor is the air left to
itself. Tripper balloons
sunsetcrawl fireblurting
indefatigably.

How it must seem up there,
downland, cornfield contours,
boundaries overlooked,
simultaneity.

It is what June makes one
believe, roomy twilight
welcoming flowerscents,
interchangeableness.

School sports day, and time for
outdoor vocal pursuits,
afternoon loudspeaker
echolaliating

the one two three of the
unseen, shrieked-at races,
hectoring vowelsurges,
incomprehensible.

On the Edge

The Westgate, Winchester

A Hampshire wall is flint, cement, lumps of chalk,
remains of other walls. If you knock it down
and strew it over the land like a dead god,
        it grows elsewhere.

And what's a town but a collection of walls
sheltering together, always unfinished,
on their way up or down? What is its history
        but buried walls?

There was a wall enclosing the city once,
until we outgrew it. Now there are only
two unclosable gates for you to pass through
        on your way in.

And this is one, a gate with a room in it.
There is always more in-between than you think,
where birds nest, or red valerian takes root
        in cracked mortar,

and there have always been gate-dwellers, people
who live in the spaces between in and out
which are as close as anyone can come to
        being nowhere.

But this was used as a prison for debtors
and drunks, for whom the world suddenly closed up
and left them face to face with the horizon,
              locked in a gate.

For them the stone was a blank page to write on,
or carve a three-masted ship, curved like a wave,
riding a scribbled sea into the distance
              beyond the wall.

But a ship's a prison too. You can't escape –
except that we have, by climbing to the roof,
where you can turn your face to the west and see
              some of outside,

or look the other way where the city dips,
then rises towards its unmarked far border.
It's been going on for ages before you came,
              but it starts here.

Under the Hill

The Great Hall, Winchester

The king sits at his table
in the meatsmoke and winelight,
the cutlery's percussion,

with a knife to cut goosemeat,
a great door closed to the wind,
his warmth in many faces,

and lets everything get cold.
Smiles congeal, gravy grows skin,
while he waits for a story.

❧

What happens when no one knocks,
no stranger is admitted
in a brief scuffle of snow,

to stand in front of the fire
and draw the ring of a sword
or ring the gold of a song?

After the last quest, the last
spell, challenge, vow and wonder,
his meat untouched, the king sleeps.

❧

And someone takes the table
from under his sleeping head
so that he's resting on air,

and paints the wrong king on it,
folds it away and hangs it
on the wall like a picture.

The fire and the wine are gone.
The hall's a box of nothing
in a wilderness of steps.

❧

He dreams he's fallen asleep
awkwardly, under the weight
of a hard wooded country,

opens his eyes in the dark
with just a splatter of light
where a stranger is waiting

to tell him one last story –
of where he's been all this time,
who he will be when he wakes.

A Ghost

The Eclipse Inn, Winchester

The drinkers outside the pub
are finishing up the last of the sunshine.
Soon it will be time to go inside and taste
 the first pint of the winter,
 the lights prickling in its foam.

Old houses have more indoors,
rooms of corners, like cupboards stuck together,
blackened woodwork hardly supporting the dark.
 Your hand can't find the light switch,
 the floor isn't where you thought.

If you stay the night, expect
to wake up at odd times, convinced it's morning,
as if you were staying several nights at once,
 to relearn all the noises
 and the textures of shadows.

And then comes a new feeling,
the slight pressure of someone looking at you.
You know the contour of warmth that people make –
 imagine it made of cold.
 There is a ghost in your room.

You see time differently now,
half-asleep. It's not a wheel or an arrow
but a house made of cupboards stuck together.
    Alice Lisle's still waiting here
    for the morning of her death.

A wind gets up in the street,
making the house lurch as if over a bump,
and she feels the world rushing through the darkness
    without hope of arriving.
    It's calm again by first light.

She steps out of the window
on to the creaking planks. The morning dazzles
after the room. Everyone's looking at her,
    expecting something from her.
    She must try to get it right.

One moment lasts for ever,
blade at the top of its arc, faces flinching,
the catch of the axeman's breath, and she can't speak
    but wants to say she's found out
    what death is: an endless now.

Strange lady – more than one ghost.
At Moyles Court she rides headless in a carriage.
We have an earlier one, still on the threshold,
    which is the place for a ghost.
    Let's leave her there, and move on.

What's Underneath

The Crypt, Winchester Cathedral

This is as much of the crypt as we can see:
a vaulted passage with a statue in it,
pillars just strong enough to hold it open,
   a blind corner at the end.
      Where does it lead?

Perhaps a store-room for unused masonry
and unlabelled bones, where leftover angels,
their faces gnawed by some parasite of stone,
   are reverting to the blocks
      they were found in.

Because underneath is the place for secrets,
for hiding botched beginnings and what's done with,
where Jane Austen's moved aside for the heating
   and the bowed figure watches
      the still-dry floor.

They built this city on water. Every year
it comes into its own again, seeping up
through the foundations into people's cellars.
   Houses nurse their inward pools
      like winter colds.

And this space is filled with reflected darkness,
chamber after chamber of underground lake
where arches meet in the middle and the crypt
    seems to be floating away
        into itself.

Dig anywhere round here and you find water.
They sent a diver down to shore up the walls
and he worked for six years in over his head
    in the cramped private ocean
        under the stones,

feeling his way among the slimy remains
of the beech-log raft that used to support them
in a blackness made of disturbed sediment –
    peat from the valley bottom
        and graveyard sludge.

Lunchtimes they would winch him up to smoke his pipe
and fill the air with the good smell of dryness.
Now his statue is up above in the light,
    and one with a bowed head guards
        what's underneath.

Sleepers

The Retrochoir, Winchester Cathedral

There is a tomb here that attracts butterflies –
    some property of the stone
        that holds the sun.

Black stone with the shape of a bishop in it.
    Space beneath, where the man was,
        Peter Des Roches,

as hard as his name now, a stone among stones,
    and mourned by no one except
        the butterflies

that seem only a nuance of the sunlight
    or the air remembering
        the way he went.

ॐ

Places have their own tombs. Asphalt and houses
    have hardened over the downs
        where he hunted

and rode out of the wood in his purple cloak
    with his men nowhere in sight
        and the stag gone

to find the country had got away from him,
    leaving a foreign hillside
        with a palace.

Welcomed among the trumpets and tapestries
    and peaches out of season,
        he somehow knew

that this was the country underneath our own
    and that his host was Arthur,
        stirring in sleep,

who gave him a small gift as a memento –
    to open his hand and make
        wings flutter out.

              ❧

Sometimes on a winter day light disturbs them
    and they fly between the white
        growths of marble,

among cut chrysanthemums and the encased
    remains of sounder sleepers
        the sun can't reach.

Off the Ground

The Triforium Gallery, Winchester Cathedral

If you could fly
this might be the place for it,
in the colonnades of air over the heads
of the walkers,

like bats unhooked
from their hanging villages
to explore the pinnacles of the chantries,
the chapel caves,

the high corners
out of the reach of dusters,
the web-blinded windows and ledges gritted
with dried-up flies,

a house so tall
flying things are at home here;
but we who have to climb stairs can cling on, too,
half off the ground.

Saints and angels,
struck from their old perches, rest
in the gallery around us, and a Bible
lies near at hand,

with dancing room
between the pages for
the red, blue and gold figures with pointed toes
and open wings.

House-Guest

Jane Austen's House, Winchester

We can't go in. There are people living here.
You may notice them sometimes moving about
behind the shine of the glass. How must they feel,
sharing their home with someone who isn't there?

Yet we think they are the ones who don't belong,
that the street is held in a Regency calm,
in the space between one clock chime and the next,
like a sentence poised at a semi-colon.

She was only staying here, and she was ill,
spending her days on the sofa, carried out
in a sedan-chair under the sun's escort
or watching the rain perform on the window.

She had been driven seventeen miles to reach
this house a street away from the cathedral
where Swithun was buried out of the weather
right on the fault-line of summer, mid-July,

which made this city the capital of rain.
And now she was here there was nothing to do
but wait for her promotion to a wheelchair
or a shelter of her own under the nave.

For two days she was more asleep than awake.
Her looks fell away. She wanted only death.
There was one last feeling she couldn't describe,
and then only her breathing left to finish.

But she is still not quite settled, our dead guest.
One feels she's only waiting for the right time,
for the visitors to stop bringing her flowers,
for the weather to change, so she can go out.

She was a desperate walker through muddy lanes,
and no one wants to stay indoors forever.
Perhaps houses are never fully lived in.
She didn't live in this. And we can't go in.

By the Forge

John Keats in Winchester

Say you had been for a walk by the river
among fields of dry yellow and brown whose smell
was baking, as if the earth were their oven,
but the afternoon was warm and cold at once
and you had noticed a numbness in the sky,
a shiver in the water, that made you yearn
for things with sun in them, apples, corn, honey.

And say the air had been fidgety today
so the gnats couldn't keep still, and overhead
it was crowded with excitable swallows.
This was your season, the time of departure.
You could feel that edge in your lungs, like the tang
of unlit bonfires or a foretaste of snow
in the last of the sunshine, as you turned back.

And you had nowhere to go now but a room
that stared at the blank side of a house, a street
you could listen to all night and hear only
the punctuation of footsteps and a cane,
so you walked through the city, where the people
had the look of those you see on holiday
as if only pretending to be themselves.

And London was waiting for you, a poem
you were almost ready to try again with.

There was another room, a woman, a book,
and a cold blur like rain you couldn't make out
from this far away. You had to be inside
writing the words before you could find their shape.
Say you were thinking of all this and standing

all of a sudden, in front of an open shop
where a basket of coals was seething orange
and a man came and stabbed it into yellow,
a cornfield of sparks. Say you watched him hammer
and thought he was beating light into a bar,
making the street dark. That's when you'd hug yourself
and say, I should like a bit of fire tonight.

The Removal

You know how sometimes
you're sitting in the house at night
when you hear a key scrape
the outside of the lock, and you're alone
expecting no one. You know how
it sounds, like a fingernail
rasping the skin of a drum.

Or you're daydreaming
over a book, thinking
you have the place to yourself
when somebody walks in
in mid-remark, as though
you'd been in the kitchen too
and had just slipped back.

You know how you're walking
along the street when the windows
switch on one after another
and you're standing suddenly
in the lightbox of a room
watching the television
over a stranger's shoulder.

And when you move house you keep
one of the keys in your pocket
and sometimes you pass the door.

You know how the moment comes
when you could walk right in
to the lounge full of staring people
and sit in the empty chair.

As if you were a ghost
or everyone else was.
As if you were on a film
and just flickering over the place
you thought you were living in –
you know what I mean. Well,
it was like that. It was like that.

Invocation

Wide wet walks where winds worry,
weedgrown web-woven wilderness,
wormy warrens, whiffling waters,

wolf way, witch world, wound
widdershins with whippy willows,
wittering with whirligig wings,

we want witness words. We waver,
wheedling, weighing, wondering.
Welcome what we whisper,

wild wood, wild wood.

Interior Designers in the Forest

A complete environment of raw furniture!
Fairly unupfront colours, brown and green,
but with strong verticals, and gaps between
to allow for the circulation of the air.
The aim is never to know quite where you are,
so it rearranges itself. This moving screen
in front of us is made of natural fern.
What do you think? Perhaps I'll just sit here
on this organic bench in the sunlight
effect. Dry rot is in, apparently.
I've seen some illusions in my time, but hey,
this place is somewhere else. And this is great –
a pond you can use for washing in, or treat
as a wild mirror. Look, a *trompe l'oeil* me!

Museum of the Forest

We drove to the forest. It was in a museum.
At the door they handed us a mudspattered map already separated
    by too much folding into its nine panels.
Chanterelles grew in the carpet. We weren't sure if they were exhibits.
We were asked to wear wellington boots to protect the mud.
We put our noses to a little hole. There was an autumn day in it,
    dry and mushroomy.
The next room was perfumed with resin, warmed by the
    greenblueyellow of an infrapine lamp.
We rolled up the sleeves of our anoraks and the prickle of rain was
    applied by tiny hypodermic syringes.
In the next room we had to leave all our sounds at the door. It
    contained the noise deer don't really make at all when they run off.
Then we were in a disorientation room with multiple paintings of
    the same tree and the sun always in the wrong position.
They locked the turnstiles half an hour ago. The cry of the last
    child has faded and the sun is setting in the north.
No one has told us if the carpet is for sleeping on.

The God of Paths

Well, now, let me see, you see these three paths.
Well, the one on the left with the bracken, you ignore that,
and the one on the right with the mud, you ignore that,
and you take the path in the middle with the acorns
until one way or another you come to a clearing – you can't miss it.
The sun will be there waiting, and a sow splutters husks.

Well, now, let me see, you see these three trees.
Well, the birch on the side of the hand you write with, you ignore
     that,
and the beech in the middle, you ignore that,
and you take the path with the mud next to the holly
on the side where you can hear your heart beating
until one way or another you come to a clearing – you can't miss it.
The sun will be getting impatient, and a pony tramps crackling.

Well, now, let me see, you see these three bushes.
Well, the sloe in the middle, you ignore that,
and the hawthorn on the side of the hand you don't write with,
     you ignore that,
and you take the path with the bracken next to the wild rose
on the side where you can't hear your heart beating
until one way or another you come to a clearing – you can't miss it.
The sun will be looking askance and fidgeting with leafspecks,
and a deer scratches its ear.

Well, now, let me see, you see these three birds.
Well, the treecreeper on the side where you can hear its heart
    beating, you ignore that,
and the siskin on the side of the hand it writes with, you ignore that,
and you take the path with the bracken and the mud and the acorns
next to the firecrest in the middle, well, if you can call it a path,
until one way or another you come to a clearing,
well, if you can call it a clearing – you can't miss it.
The sun will have given up and gone home, and the sounds you hear
may be a sow spluttering husks or a pony tramping crackling or a
    deer scratching its ear,
but I shouldn't like to bet on it. That's where I live, but I'm out at
    the moment.
I'll get back to you. You can't miss me, or, at least,
one way or another, I can't miss you.

The Ornamental Hermit

Not really ornamental, a white figure
you might glimpse from the drive, deep in the beech woods,
as you were making your way towards the house,
standing so still he might have been a long strip
of sunlight on the bark, except that you felt,
not his eyes on you exactly, but his *thoughts*.

Hardly anyone saw him close up. The cook,
who had, said he was wearing a floppy robe
of coarse stuff and looked like a man in a bag,
and a visitor who had come face to face
with what appeared to be a nightgowned person
supposed he was mad or walking in his sleep.

No one could agree on his age. The footman
who left last night's jellied fowl and potatoes
beside his sandbank grotto in the morning
would say, after a long pause, he thought the chap
wore spectacles but he stayed in the shadows
hunched over his Bible. They were not to speak.

He was a lover who had renounced the world
or else he had been promised a thousand pounds
if he could live for seven years in the cave
that had been scooped out for him, rising at dawn,
then brooding the whole day over the hourglass,
at night praying or reading by candlelight.

Hermits were all the rage these days but this one
could not have been laid on as an ornament
for houseparties. Some of the guests went so far
as to doubt his existence, or at least claimed
that he had long ago climbed the wall, leaving
his implements in the slowly filling hole.

But it was like this. There are times when a man
must grasp where he is living. It's not enough
any more to lie under your roof at night
hearing the dry rain, to own all those acres
of dark and dirt, without someone to feel it,
to be in the thick. That's what I paid him for.

St Catherine and the Philosophers

This is a painting with five books in it.
The young woman stands with her back to the philosophers
who have their backs to the window. They are reading,
ignoring the passers-by who are reading them.
Behind them all we can see the rest of the palace,
a harbour, a mountain, the landscape going blue.

The first book is a guide to Purgatory,
the spiral mountain. The only escape is up,
but you have to know the way. This book will tell you.
It takes three men to read it, and first of all
you need the guide to the book. It's in your hand,
uncrumple it. Or you could just turn round
and see if you can untwist the rocks themselves.

The second is the book of Good and Evil.
If you read two pages at once you get the world
exactly as it is. The red and black
figures twitch into life as you flicker through them.

The third book was originally a baby
but a sorceress appeared at his christening
and turned his skin to leather and his cries
to hieroglyphs. No one has told the priest,
or else he blesses it anyway, not knowing
what happens when it grows up, in Chapter 20.

The fourth book is so real that Catherine holds it
in an insulating cloth. It gives the low-down
on the philosophers, how without looking
they can tell everything about the world
except what she is doing there. She knows.

The fifth is the perfect book. It is written
in a language only it can understand,
but it's bored with reading itself. It lies around
yawning all day, leaving itself undone.

The king and the man he talks to have given up books.
There is so much else for them to do, hill walking,
crowd control, sailing, palace architecture.
The king explains that he has hired a sculptor
to describe the future in a marble frieze
above their heads. No one has read it yet,
and even Catherine doesn't know that the wheel
in that little panel up there has her name on it.

Nest of Devils

When we moved into the old house
we found a nest of devils in the cellar,
like cats with horns and covered in red fur.

They were too fast to catch.
You had to watch their spiked tails,
and one of them gave me a painful bite.

It was only defending its young, I suppose,
the little devils. Their eyes weren't open yet.
At night the mother devil sang to them.

There was always a lot of noise in that cellar.
They spoke Latin or some language
that was all long words and clanging sounds,

like dropping something heavier than aitches.
Sometimes they came upstairs at night
and we heard them whispering on the landing.

A man from the council came but they liked the poison.
A priest came and told them to get behind him,
and a few Hell's Angels came to worship them.

We thought they'd lower the value of the house.
They were a fire risk, anyway. Sometimes
things burst into flame when they touched them,

but they always looked guilty. (Or was that just their colour?)
I used to think they were trying to communicate.
They would stare very hard and wave their pitchforks.

And then one morning they were gone.
Perhaps the cellar got too cold for them
or too many people had told them to go to hell.

But some nights I pause as I pass the cellar
thinking maybe the species has been misunderstood,
and what if right now I smelt brimstone behind the door –

would I be tempted to leave them there? You know, I think I would.

Spending the Night in the Temple

> Many dreams, they accepted, were 'heaven-sent' . . . The gods
> themselves spoke directly with the dreamer . . . Dreams were courted
> deliberately in temples with special 'incubatory' chambers, from the
> Britons' Lydney in Kent to the great centres at Pergamum and Aigai
> in Asia.
>
> ROBIN LANE FOX, *Pagans and Christians*

As we walk up the hill the sun carries on setting
as for a normal night. We enter the precincts
almost a crowd and knock with its last red on
a small door that shelters in a great one.

We test the spaces with our footsteps,
small ones and great ones, dimnesses
that harden in the torchlight.

This room feels full of us.
Non-noise of blankets.

The settling place.

٭

We can still manage some horizontal courtesies,
a handshake blanket to blanket, half of a smile
with the rest nowhere, hallos into the dark.
The high priest enters with his head agleam

and we receive him sprawling in state
like sick children. We are welcome.
Day will be served in due course.

Now it's time for goodnight.
Lights turn to smoke smell

and eyelid fire.

        ❧

In the time it takes to turn over, wrench a pillow
and colonize it, there is a polite space left
for afterwords, and then the grunts of bodies
taking us back inside them for the night.

So it's up to me. Snubbed by the dark
and its competitive breathing
I try to remember how.

We're sharing with pigeons.
Undertone gargles,

feather wrestling.

        ❧

Here if at all, now if at all, the god will visit
wearing white as usual and speaking in riddles
because we've used up all the sensible words.
He has his own light so he lives in this.

He has my pain at his fingertips,
my love-life worn next to his skin,
my money in his pocket.

Now I must go to sleep,
and he may appear

when I have gone.

လ

And a swimming elephant rears up out of the sea
and walks through the village on its hind legs. It wears
a white toga and has an interpreter
to blare its wishes through a bronze trumpet.

*Do not be afraid. I only want
to use your villa for the night.*
I hide in a burnt-out house.

Cold air through the window.
The great trunk feeling

for the small key.

လ

A road that isn't a road, flowers that have no smell.
Their shapes are too simple and my hand goes through them.
It isn't countryside, it's a foreign world.
A chariot draws up with four young men

in white leather jerkins, with greased-back
black hair. They all have the same face
but I get in anyway.

As we drive off, the face
hardens and flattens

to a serpent's.

&

It will be all right if I can only find my wool cloak.
It was a thick white one. I saw a man just now
who'd seen it in Apulia recently.
I have no money so I have to walk.

I get to the harbour and they say
no entry without a wool cloak,
and this man is wearing it,

and I say let me in,
that's mine, and besides

my back's freezing.

&

I wake on the cold floor. It's raining in the distance.
There is enough daylight to see the people now.
They lie where sleep has thrown them, wreaths of blankets
clutched between limbs. It's like a massacre.

One walks naked in the marketplace,
one tries to run through sticky air,
one steps from a high tower.

This room's buzzing with dreams.
What if mine were meant

for someone else?

⁂

The trumpet is the god's voice, the elephant his might.
The villa is this in-between place, his temple.
The key is to unlock you, but if you try
to ride beside him he is venomous.

Walk under the rain like a poor man
without a coat to keep you dry.
You've seen some of his faces.

Be proud. Pay as you leave.
I will pray for you.

Use the small door.

Going Through the Villages

Midnight Faring
Slow-under-Wool
Settle Down
Wallow

Lullaby Lea
Lullaby Lea

Long Reckoning
Tremble Noctis
Market Looming
Venge

Lullaby Lea
Lullaby Lea

Sheep's Quorum
Inward Haven
Gossip-sub-Breathing
Glimmerfields

Wanders End
Wanders End

Twentieth-Century Dream

1900–1909   I am in a darkened lecture-hall
watching a magic lantern picture
of my own head. We are all
analysing my thoughts. Freud is there,
so we watch carefully as the scene
becomes the dust and flames of a war.
As oxcarts roll, you can see my brain
turning the images into neat
haiku-like poems. What do they mean,
Freud asks, try to remember. But

1910–1919   I am setting off on a journey
in a great rush of snow to the pole.
Captain Scott is trudging beside me
when his boot gets stuck. He tries to pull
and the whole foot comes off. A band plays
'Abide with Me' as I watch him topple
into the wet. Then I realize
everyone's come unstuck. I'm walking in
a soup of legs, hands and rolling eyes
that they call Nobody's Land. And then

1920–1929   a long time passes. I'm at a dance:
Cubist dresses in liqueur colours,
smoke in the air and the musicians
playing tin cans and old newspapers.
I can't find out who's paying for this

but it's been the cocktail hour for years
and they haven't called time. The police
keep raiding, but so does Al Capone.
I'm chatting up a girl who says yes,
yes, she will, endlessly. Whereupon

1930–1939   I wake up. I'm sitting in my room
in Oxbridge in a stodgy armchair.
I want to get up, but I don't seem
to be able to move a finger.
I've come adrift inside my body
and will have to sit here forever
with Auden's poems, the cold Earl Grey,
the apostle spoons, and the china,
listening for footsteps, one, two, three,
floorboard, doorknob, he'll be here in a

1940–1949   tic and a flick of hair and a shout.
The man on the platform is Chaplin,
the Great Director, who makes them cut
with a lifted palm. Some blonde women
with heroes' shoulders are singing of
blitzkrieg, but when I try to join in
I can't speak the language, and I have
a star on my forehead so they know
I'm in the wrong film. I start to leave
but then the whole world explodes. Somehow

1950–1959   I make it home. My ideal wife
can get the best out of a vacuum

and looks like a hen in her headscarf.
Every man on our block has the same
haircut and it makes me suspicious.
I watch their eyes on the train. They seem
to be watching me back. The voices
on the TV carry on after
I turn it off. Sergeant Bilko is
probably a red plant. Remember

1960–1969   where you were? I was in the attic
with Che, Marilyn, Mick. The walls were
hung with Vietnam posters. We took
a cactus each and I waited for
the spikes to take hold. Now I feel weird.
It's as if everything is the colour
it always was. When I go outside
there are cars and people who are like
working. I'm feeling so clear-headed,
like not being in a dream. I look

1970–1979   down the street and there are the banners
flaring above the trestle tables,
the spilled paper cups, plates of afters,
and no one in sight. A tabloid falls
at my feet and I read the headline,
which means nothing to me: Bondage Rules!
Where is the disco? Johnny Rotten
promised to smash it up. It gets dark
as I wait for something to happen.
None of the lights come on. Meanwhile, back

at the office, the cheeseplants are now
so enormous my desk vanishes
in a jigsaw of jungle. I go
trekking through open-plan wilderness
to tell Office Services but just
as I reach the door a storm crashes
through the foliage. PCs are tossed
in a shower of bits through the air,
and crunch underfoot. I get out fast
and steer the Porsche for Port Stanley. Here

I am now, inside my darkened head.
The dream is over. This is the post-dream:
birds singing, cars passing in the road,
my own breath. Soon I'll know who I am,
I'll know when I am. That is the post
landing on the doormat. The alarm
will go off in a minute. The last
blur of sleep will clear. In a minute
a hundred years has gone, and the past
is all a dream, and I wake from it.